CORN SNAKES AS PETS

A GUIDE TO KEEPING AND RAISING CORN SNAKES

JACQUELINE SILVERDALE

CONTENTS

INTRODUCTION

Choosing a pet for yourself or your child is always a tough decision and it is fantastic that you have decided to thoroughly do your research before deciding on getting a corn snake. My goal with this book is to talk you through the immensely exciting journey of being a corn snake owner for the first time. I'll provide you with plenty of information and guidance and also make sure you have considered all the potential implications and downsides of owning such a pet.

Owning any snake for the first time involves a lot of preparation and planning. You may have chosen to get a reptile because you heard they can be left alone for a week while you are on holiday and that they are very easy to care for. While these facts are both true, there is also a lot involved in making sure that you have a healthy and happy pet, so please be sure to read the information in this book carefully before you decide that if a corn snake is the perfect pet for you.

In fact, your preparation should start at least a few weeks before the arrival of your new snake and throughout that time there is a lot to consider. Creating a safe and healthy environment, getting all the essential equipment and food prepared in advance, educating everyone in the household on proper husbandry tips and making sure that for the first few days of your snake's arrival, they can be comfortably left in peace to acclimatize to their new surroundings. All of this will need to be planned in advance, regardless of which reptile or snake that you choose. And, while some of the advice you'll receive is the same for all breeds, there are certain things you need to make sure you have in place particularly for corn snakes.

Although they are widely recognized to be an extremely easy breed to care for, there are still certain basic requirements that will need to be carefully considered before you bring your snake home. In this book, I will spend a lot of time looking at exactly what those requirements are, why they are so important and how to make sure you keep on top of your day to day duties as a responsible pet owner.

None of this is intended to put you off - as you will see in this book, there are fantastic benefits to choosing this type of pet. Assuming you adequately prepare for the arrival of your snake and you pay careful attention to my tips about how to handle the first few weeks of having your new pet in your home, you will very quickly be able to enjoy playing with your snake, handling them, making them part of your home and getting to know their personality. And, if you are anything like me, you will find that this is the first of many corn snakes you will bring home over the years because, once you learn the basics and get used to being a snake owner, it is a fantastic hobby and opens you up to a very supportive and interactive reptile enthusiast community.

As you prepare to welcome your new member to the family, let me help you cover all the bases and offer some handy hints and tips on how to make this a smooth and enjoyable process. I have intentionally designed this book with the whole family in mind and I often make reference to how to educate and help young children take care of and enjoy their new pet. It is very important to note though that even if you are buying your corn snake as a pet for your children to enjoy and you are delegating the feeding, cleaning and caring tasks to them - a responsible adult needs to ensure best practices and careful handling at all times. Small changes in a snake's environment can be damaging and traumatic to the snake and improper handling and lack of care and attention can lead to an unhappy snake and even occasionally small bites. It is very easy to avoid this and ensuring you stick to the main guidelines in this book will ensure you have a happy, healthy, active and playful corn snake for years to come.

In this book, you will learn the basics of corn snake ownership, how to keep your corn snake healthy and happy, how to ensure you stay on the right side of all your legal obligations as a pet owner and how to reach out to the wider reptile enthusiast community when you want to share your experiences or ask further questions. I will at times list other sites, publications or informative links of interest and I will aim to provide you with relevant details based on your location. For our readers outside the US and Europe, I would encourage you to try and find the equivalent information for your home region.

I have also tried to include as much information as possible as to where you should select the best materials for the cage, as well as the best places to get feed and substrate, but again this will depend on your location. I have tried to give you much more general advice as to what to look for in each of these cases, to provide you with the tools to make smarter decisions while shopping.

As with all pet ownership, new and improved products will come on the market and sometimes even the best practice guidelines for caring for your animal may change. It is important therefore to see this book as your gateway to a continuous learning program of corn snake ownership and ensure that you are updating your knowledge and skills as a pet owner on a regular basis. You might be surprised at just how much is involved in caring for your tiny new family member, but I promise that it will be an enjoyable journey and you will find the answers to all your burning questions over the next few pages as I take you through every facet of being a responsible corn snake owner.

Thank you for making this your reference guide for your new venture into snake ownership. I look forward to being a part of your journey. Let's get started!

CHAPTER ONE: GETTING TO KNOW YOUR CORN SNAKE

B efore we begin learning how to take care of your corn snake in your home, let's spend some time getting to know the origins of the corn snake, how it acts in its natural environment and why it has risen to become one of the most popular snake breeds for pet ownership. Even though corn snakes have been domesticated for years, it is still very insightful to learn and understand as much as you can about the natural habitat that your animal is used to. As well as helping you design and maintain the perfect cage environment, it is also useful for the general awareness of your snake's behaviors in order to better monitor its overall health.

THE ORIGIN **Of Corn Snakes**

First, let us look at the actual origin of the name itself. All animals are grouped into species and subspecies depending on their defining characteristics, changes in their evolution and other distinctive differences. The name 'corn snake' is a colloquial term that was used to distinguish this particular breed of snake based on their appearance and other subtle and sometimes not so subtle differences from other snakes. Their actual Latin name is Pantherophis Guttatus and they belong to the Colubridae family of snake, which is generalized by non-venomous, rear-fanged snakes. Even within the Colubridae Family, there are other smaller families and the corn snake belongs to one known as Colubrinae. More commonly called the 'rat snake; family, it also represents milk snakes, vine snakes and indigo snakes, but it could be argued that the corn snake is certainly the most well known of the rat snake family.

Corn Snakes Are Hardy Animals

When it comes to learning more about their natural habitat, this particular family of snakes is known for being resilient across a whole host of habitats. They are found in mountainous regions and rocky terrain, but are as equally at home in damp environments and even swampland. Due to their flexibility and ease with which they adapt to new environments, they are also more likely to be found in abandoned buildings, farms and even in suburban areas. Corn snakes, in particular, like to hide in covered areas during the day and would not be one of the most commonly found snakes to be out in the open in the wild. They have a relatively short life span in the wild and most do not make it to adulthood. This is also important to remember that once they have been in captivity, there is no chance they would survive in the wild either, so it's probably not a good idea to try and 'free' them!

Considering their propensity to hide under rocks and be particularly anti-social, it is surprising then that, in captivity, corn snakes can actually be very active and friendly pets. Because of this, they are easily one of the most popular reptile pet choices. Distinguishable by their bright colors, it is thought that the name 'corn snake' actually derived from the similarities between their checkerboard style underbelly and some patterns of kernels of corn. It is more likely, however, that they got their name by the fact that they would sometimes prey on rats and mice in newly harvested corn and were a common site around grain farms. However they got their name, they are certainly one of the easiest snakes to identify, thanks to their bright and often unusual patterns. As a rule, they are calm, non-aggressive and very easy to care for, which makes them an excellent choice of pet, particularly if you have young children in the household.

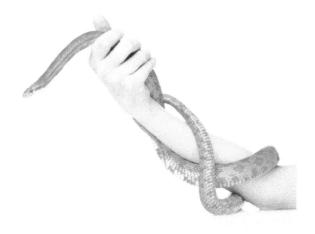

They have a lifespan of around 6-8 years and remain relatively small, although some can grow up to 5 feet long. They are characteristically non-aggressive, but if you are buying a very young snake, expect a few small bites if they are feeling threatened or under stress while they adapt to their new home environment. If you are buying the snake for your children, it is important to be aware of this fact and be extra vigilant if your children are handling the snake. However, if you follow my guidelines in this book on how to properly introduce your new snake to the tank and to your home, you will have a calm, relaxed and happy snake.

Pet Snakes Require Special Care

As I have already stated, although your children can be the ones to love and play with the snake, it does require an adult to make sure that all the snake's needs are met, so please be responsible when it comes to ensuring that adequate food, water and living conditions are provided. I will go into this in much more detail in later chapters where I talk about handling, preparing for and caring for your corn snake. Corn snakes love to explore and enjoy getting attention. As they grow, they will prove to be fantastic and loving pets, as long as you take the time to integrate them into their new environment and follow the handling and feeding procedures that I will talk about later in the book.

Corn snakes mate in the spring and then lay their eggs in the summer, so you can use this as a guide for when it is best to buy your snake, depending on what age and size of snake you prefer. Due to the overwhelming popularity of this type of snake as a pet though, you will be almost always guaranteed to find snakes available for you to give a home to. Regardless of what sex of snake you buy, they should never be kept in a cage with another snake or reptile. Snakes are solitary creatures and being kept in close proximity to another animal, even another corn snake, will cause them huge anxiety.

Advanced Topics

If your plan is to become a snake breeder, a topic which I have covered later in this book, it is strongly advised that you do much more research and study in this area. The aim of this book is to prepare you for corn snake ownership, so for anything relating to advanced topics, like breeding, it is recommended that you do further research.

Corn Snakes Require A Special Diet

Like most reptiles, your corn snake lives on a diet of mice and, in the wild, they will sometimes snack on other small animals, like baby chicks or small rats. One advantage the corn snake has over other popular breeds, such as the ball python is that even when they are fully grown, they can still get enough sustenance from a diet of only mice. Problems can arise with other snakes when they need to move on to rats as they grow, so this is another reason that the corn snake is one of the easiest breeds to care for.

What a corn snake eats and how they need to be fed is an important consideration when determining whether a snake is actually the right type of pet for you. Pet shops and suppliers make it very easy to feed your snake rodents by selling feeders, which are small, frozen rodents that you can buy, thaw and then place in your snake's tank. Your snake will only eat once a week and it is actually preferable to feed them frozen mice and rats to avoid potential injury from eating live prey. For some families and in some situations this might not be ideal, so please take the time to consider if you and anyone caring for the snake is going to be comfortable with this process. Again, this is something I will go into in a lot more detail on later in the book, but if you really can't stand the thought of dealing with either live or frozen rodents, I may have just have saved you a few chapters of reading and you may need to think about a different type of pet! Snakes are most definitely carnivores and they eat their food whole, which can be a fascinating process to witness - but it might be a good idea to check out some examples of this on YouTube first, before committing to the entire process happening weekly in a glass cage in your home.

Still here? Fantastic! As you get to know more about the hardiness and adaptability of these animals you will certainly build an appreciation for what a resilient species they are. In this chapter, I have covered just a few general notes about the corn snake, but there are plenty more fascinating facts that I will cover later in the book. I will also talk often about snake and reptile breeds in general and it can be very helpful for you to research other breeds if you like. The most important thing is you get a pet that you are completely happy with and that fits in with your life. And if you are sure that pet is a snake, I couldn't think of a better place to start than with a corn snake.

CHAPTER SUMMARY

In this chapter, we have learned:

- The corn snake is a member of the Colubridae family, most commonly referred to as the Rat Snake family
- How the corn snake got its unusual name and the proper Latin term for the species
- About the corn snake's natural habitat, why they are so resilient and where in the wild they are most commonly found
- Handy facts about the corn snake, including what they eat, when the breeding season is and how well they interact with other snakes

IN THE NEXT CHAPTER, you will learn:

- Some important points to keep in mind before choosing your corn snake
- How to know for sure that this is the best pet for you and your family and what questions you should be asking in anticipation of deciding a snake is the best pet for you
- Key facts about the Corn snake, how to handle them and what to expect from owning one as a pet
- How to make sure you are prepared for what is ahead as a responsible corn snake owner
- Tips and tricks for helping younger children prepare for the new member to the family and how to make sure that they enjoy their new pet for years to come

CHAPTER TWO: BEFORE YOU BUY

How do you know if a corn snake is the right pet for you and your family? As with all purchases of animals, it is crucially important to do your homework and learn all you can about the animal in advance. One advantage to the corn snake being one of the most popular snake breeds to own is that there is a wealth of information and general husbandry tips online that really take you through the pros and potential cons of owning such an animal.

Handling Snakes

Once you have done your research online, the next stage should be to talk to some fellow corn snake owners and ask them questions about the general care of the snake, as well as anything they wish they had known before they purchased. You should also try and handle some corn snakes in advance. Although they are particularly calm and non-aggressive snakes, they do have a reputation for being harder to handle than larger breeds, mostly due to their active nature and their love of exploring. If you are bringing home a baby corn snake, expect it to be quite a lot of work to make sure it doesn't escape from your hold. You should also be extremely careful when allowing young children to handle the baby snakes, as they can be extremely delicate.

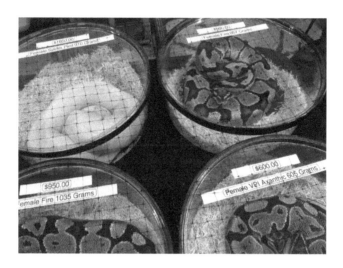

These aren't the usual prices of corn snakes! Apologies for the sticker shock!

A FANTASTIC WAY TO meet and get to know other corn snake owners and reptile enthusiasts is to check out the many pet expos or reptile showcases that happen in the major cities throughout the US. And, through research online and the forums and informative websites with community engagement platforms, you can also find a lot of fellow reptile owners even further afield. If you do not live in the US, you can check online for similar events happening in a region near you and it is always a great idea to become a regular at your local pet store.

One advantage that corn snakes have over other snake breeds is their hardy nature. As a beginner snake owner, it will be expected that you make a few mistakes. It is only natural that as you get used to your new routine, you may overextend a feeding window or not have the tank set up as recommended. The good news is that corn snakes are more adaptable than other breeds and will recover quickly from suboptimal conditions. That is never an excuse for neglecting your corn snake or not remedying problems immediately, but it at least gives the novice pet owner a bit of a learning window within which mistakes can be made. With some other snake and reptile breeds, even the smallest changes to conditions could prove harmful to the animal.

TEMPERAMENT

Even though the corn snake is widely recognized to be the best choice as a starter snake, there are always some downsides to consider when choosing this as your pet. Particularly if this is your first snake, you have to make sure that this is the right decision for you. As mentioned before, corn snakes can be particularly flighty when handled. They are normally very docile and calm creatures, but every snake has its own personality and if you have a particularly active snake that loves to explore, it can be hard to control. Corn snakes are built smaller, thinner and are slippier to handle than other breeds of snake. They love to wrap around objects and are always on the move, which is great if you love an active pet, but definitely something to consider if you are buying a reptile because you imagine them to be slower.

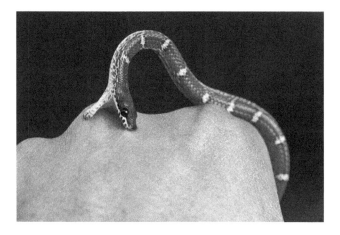

BITING

Particularly when they are young, corn snakes can be prone to small bites, but this is a natural consideration regardless of what animal you buy. Your snake will only bite if it feels threatened and, when you consider the size of the corn snake in relation to yourself or other members of the family that may be handling it, it can be understandable why they would get stressed. Young children have a tendency to be unaware of how gentle they need to be when handling delicate animals, which is why it is vitally important that you monitor all interactions to ensure the safety of both the snake and the child. The great thing about corn snakes though is they are so small that even if they do bite it will be very painless and not traumatic - unlike larger snakes or other reptiles. Also, remember that they are completely non-venomous, so there is no danger in getting a small bite. If you do experience this, the first thing to remember is not to reprimand the snake, as this will only make the situation worse. Animals don't have a language to tell us when they are feeling distressed and, particularly for snakes, the only method they have at their disposal if they cannot escape danger is to use their teeth.

How To Purchase A Corn Snake

When you are thinking about purchasing your new pet, you will need to make a choice between buying from a breeder, a pet shop or adopting a rescue snake. Remember at all times that you are buying a live animal, so purchasing from less than reputable breeders or suppliers is NOT recommended. Please do your research - there are some fantastic online breeders out there, but make sure you build a relationship with them and ensure all delivery processes are secure and comfortable for the snake. Because corn snakes are so readily available and such a popular choice, unfortunately, a lot of them become neglected and abandoned, so if you feel able to give a corn snake a calm and loving home, you can look into one of the many rescue services in your area.

CHAPTER SUMMARY

In this chapter, we have learned:

- Some important points to keep in mind before choosing your corn snake
- How to know for sure that this is the best pet for you and your family and what questions you should be asking in anticipation of deciding a snake is the best pet for you
- Key facts about the corn snake, how to handle them and what to expect from owning one as a pet
- How to make sure you are prepared for what is ahead as a responsible corn snake owner
- Tips and tricks for helping younger children prepare for the new member to the family and how to make sure that they enjoy their new pet for years to come

IN THE NEXT CHAPTER, you will learn:

- How to set up your cage properly to make your new arrival feel even more at home
- Why the environment is so important to the health of your snake and how to monitor and control the environment for optimum conditions
- How to pick the best substrate for your corn snake and the most important additions to the cage to make your snake happy and healthy

CHAPTER THREE: PREPARING FOR YOUR CORN SNAKE

Y ou want to make sure your snake can get settled into their new environment straight away, so you should start the process of preparing their home 2-3 weeks prior. The tank should be fully set up and at the right temperature for at least a few days before arrival. If you have young children, involve them in this process - it can be a fun exercise to design the new cage. There are so many accessories available on the market and you can be as creative as you like, but there are several key components that you must install in order to ensure a happy pet.

Vivariums

IF YOU ARE BRINGING HOME a baby corn snake, chances are they will be only a few inches long. Over the first two years of their life, they will gradually grow to adult size. You can expect your corn snake to measure between 2.5 - 5 feet long when fully grown, so please keep this in mind when purchasing a vivarium for it to live in. Vivariums come in all shapes and sizes and a small plastic one will suffice while the snake is still a baby, but when it grows, you should purchase at least a 20-gallon long aquarium. Please also remember to purchase clamps for the lid of your tank - corn snakes can escape through the smallest of spaces and are very hard to find if they go missing.

WITHIN THE TANK, you need to make sure that your snake has enough water. If you live in an area with good tap water, this will be sufficient or else you can use conditioned water. Also, ensure that it is neither too hot nor too cold - room temperature is perfect. Water bowls should be big enough for the snake to fit in fully coiled without the water pouring out the sides. There are two main reasons for this - your snake will use the water to ease in its shedding process and increasing the size of the water bowl to fit the snake as it grows will ensure an adequate level of humidity in the tank. Your corn snake might also like to poop in the water bowl, rather than on its dry bedding. As long as all bowel movements are regular and your snake is healthy, this isn't anything to worry about and the water should just be cleaned regularly.

HEATING THE TANK

When it comes to heating the tank, you should use a heating pad or heat tape, in conjunction with a lamp. The heat pad or heat tape should be placed on the underside of the tank in only one corner and should not measure more than one third the size of the tank. The reason for putting the heat pad on only one side of the tank is so that your snake can move away from it or towards it, based on their level of comfort and heat-seeking.

Bear in mind that snakes are ectothermic and cannot heat or cool themselves without an external source, so you are completely responsible for ensuring it can always maintain a healthy temperature for itself and avoid extremes of hot or cold at all times. Even heat pads can be ineffective, so it is best to always use a thermometer in the tank so you can monitor the temperature. Keeping the tank at an even 80 degrees Fahrenheit is optimal, but anything between 75 and 85 is acceptable.

Always avoid putting the tank in direct sunlight, as this can cause the tank to become overheated very quickly and could hurt or even kill your snake. It is also important that your snake maintains a nearly 12-hour day and night cycle. In the wild, these snakes are crepuscular, which means they are very active around twilight, so they rely on the natural day and night cycle. You should try and replicate this cycle as much as possible and be careful of using the room that your snake is in throughout the night or leaving lights on that might disrupt their pattern.

Corn snakes are very adaptable and resilient, so don't worry if you notice a problem or that conditions in the tank have not been optimal. Just make sure you correct it promptly and then monitor your snake to ensure their comfort.

Bedding And Substrate

Corn snakes in particular love to burrow, so making sure that their tank is filled with dry bedding is very important. Depending on where you live, there will be popular brands and you should always consult with your local pet shop or snake breeder to see what they suggest. In the US, aspen bedding proves particularly popular amongst snake owners.

While there are a lot of great bedding options available, there are some types that should not be used for your corn snake. Cedar and pine shavings are not suitable and, as your corn snake is a burrowing snake, you should also avoid carpeting or sand. Sand can be particularly harmful if ingested, but keep in mind the environments that snakes come from and, as long as the overall environment is safe and healthy and you provide adequate light, water and heat, ingesting small amounts of sand, dirt or other loose earth will not cause major problems for your corn snake. Reptile expos are also a great way to learn about which brands are best, as well as pick up some important tips for keeping your snakes environment safe, clean and enjoyable as they grow.

Hides

Within the tank, your snake will need two hides - one dry and one humid, which can be created very easily and give the snake vital areas to shed, as well as hide. For the humid hide, start by taking a small container and cutting a hole in it to allow your snake easy access in and out. Then, fill the tub with wet moss, such as sphagnum or peat moss. This can be purchased easily from any pet store. Dampen it slightly before putting it into the humid hide. Check this regularly, as it will dry out easily in the tank. You can also put dry moss in other areas of the tank if you wish, but in the humid hide, your snake should always have a damp environment that is separate from the rest of the dry areas in the tank. In general, corn snakes require very low humidity, so please ensure that the rest of their tank remains dry.

Decoration

When it comes to the decoration of the tank, there are numerous videos on YouTube that might provide some inspiration for designing an eye-catching environment. You can use visuals on the inside of the tank to provide an interesting backdrop and you can have lots of fun creating a playground for your snake. Your corn snake loves to hide and explore, so the more unique and interesting the surroundings the better!

Please remember if you are introducing any type of wood or other material from outside, it needs to be disinfected thoroughly before being introduced to your tank. Wood and bark, in particular, can be filled with parasites which, in an enclosed environment, can be deadly for your snake. All items should be soaked and disinfected with bleach, then thoroughly rinsed and dried before putting in the tank. Also, remember if you are using any type of silicone or glue for the design or backdrop of your tank, this all must be left to air out for a few days before introducing your snake. A good rule of thumb is to place your head inside the tank and, if you can smell any trace of chemicals, it needs to air out for longer.

TEMPERATURE REGULATION

Once you have decorated and fitted your tank with the essentials, there are a few important additions that you need to make in order to be able to monitor the health of your snake. Monitoring the temperature of the tank is extremely important, as your snake has no way to regulate its body temperature. That is why having a heat source at only one side of the tank is so important - the idea being that if the snake wants to cool down, it simply has to move to the other side of the tank. However, if the heat pad malfunctions, it is too large or if the tank is in the direct sunlight, there could be a serious problem. In such an enclosed environment, it takes no time at all for the temperature to increase to the level of being harmful or even deadly for your pet. We obviously want to avoid this at all costs, so let's take some time to review some monitoring options for the tank. I'll also cover how you can instantly spot discomfort with your corn snake, so you can notice if they are obvious distress, allowing you to react much quicker.

One of the most common ways to monitor the temperature inside your snake's cage is through the use of adhesive thermometer strips. These are long strips that are applied vertically to the inside of the cage and basically look like a standard thermometer, in the form of a flat adhesive. As the temperature changes, the various parts of the thermometer glow and the colors change to represent the cooling and heating. These strips are normally staged in five-degree increments, however, so although they give a great overall representation of the health of the snake's environment, it is much more advisable to use a more specific device, like a digital probe thermometer.

A digital thermometer works by placing the probe somewhere inside the snake's cage. The probe connects to a digital display that you keep on the outside of the cage. These are much more accurate than an adhesive thermometer, as they reflect the actual temperature inside the cage. Get into the habit of regularly testing and calibrating your digital thermometer and probe to ensure it is working. You can do this easily by placing the probe in ice water and checking that the readout is 32 degrees Fahrenheit / 0 degrees Celsius. It should be sufficient to do this every month or two, but, between calibration events, be sure to keep an eye on the temperature readout. It should be easy to spot any abnormalities and adjust accordingly.

Bioactive Enclosures

Bioactive enclosures are growing in popularity and, as well as providing a very comfortable environment for your snake, they can also be fun to grow and provide a colorful addition to any room. Bioactive vivariums are based on the concept of recreating a microcosm of the snake's natural habitat and are both self-containing and self-sustaining. It is a living enclosure with small invertebrates, such as earthworms and millipedes, whose purpose is to decompose the natural waste within the enclosure. Referred to as the 'cleanup crew' for this reason, within a fully functioning bioactive vivarium, there is no need to clean the tank and the other flora and fauna contribute to the ecosystem.

AS A BRAND NEW SNAKE OWNER, it is probably advisable to start with a regular tank, but if you want to work up to a bioactive tank as your snake grows, there are multiple options for how to achieve this in a way that works with your lifestyle and budget. Due to the natural growth of plants and life within the tank, it is aesthetically pleasing and also very educational to watch a bioactive ecosystem grow and operate over time. It also provides your corn snake with as natural an environment as possible, which makes for a happier and more comfortable snake.

CHAPTER SUMMARY

In this chapter, we have learned:

- How to set up your cage properly to make your new arrival feel even more at home
- Why the environment is so important to the health of your snake and how to monitor and control the environment for optimum conditions
- How to pick the best substrate for your corn snake and what the most important additions to the cage are to make your snake happy and healthy

IN THE NEXT CHAPTER, you will learn:

- What to keep in mind when bringing your corn snake home
- How to handle your corn snake and what are the most important things to remember before handling
- What you should feed your corn snake and how to manage this process
- Important facts to remember about handling and feeding with particular reference to the first week of bringing your snake home

CHAPTER FOUR: BRINGING YOUR CORN SNAKE HOME

Congratulations! You are now the proud owner of your first corn snake and you will now be excited about bringing them home and getting them settled into their new environment. By now, you should have your tank or vivarium ready. It should be at the correct temperature and there should be a full water bowl, two hides and adequate bedding for your new arrival.

FOR THE FIRST week or two, it's important to remember not to overwhelm your corn snake as they try and settle into their new home. Depending on how you purchased the snake, it may have had a traumatic journey in getting to your home - particularly if it was shipped rather than hand-delivered. It is always an exciting event welcoming a new member to your household and it is great to involve the whole family, but try to keep the welcoming process as calm and smooth as possible. Especially if you are buying a baby snake, it can be a scary process for them and they will need some time to settle. If you have young children, it will be beneficial to sit them down and explain this process with them. Building a good relationship with their new pet is extremely important and you want to make sure that they don't get bored with the early process of allowing the snake some settling-in time. After that, they will have a happy, active pet for years to come, so it's worth making sure this early period goes well!

Allowing Your Snake To Acclimate

When your snake first arrives in your home, the most important thing is to make sure they can acclimatize straight away. This is why they must be left alone for at least 5 - 7 days. This means no handling, no interaction, no tapping the glass and no changes to the environment, like being moved into different rooms in the house. The only thing you need to ensure throughout this time is that fresh water is available daily. As you remove and then replace the water bowl in the tank, you must be extra careful to make it a slow and steady process with no sudden movements. Don't put your hand near your snake and don't attempt to touch it and especially don't try to pick them up.

Reptile's brains are structured differently from mammals and temperature and environment play a crucial part in their overall health and wellbeing. If you don't stick to this advice for the first week, you could inflict lasting damage on your relationship with your new snake and you may find that you have an aggressive and unfriendly pet. And, I can't stress this enough - if you have young children, it is vitally important that they are aware of the reasons for this process also.

After the first week, you can start to slowly begin interacting with your snake and you can also start to think about their first feed. First of all, let's look at how to make sure your corn snake is ready for handling and note the important points to remember about this part of the process.

Handling

If your snake bites or is obviously distressed, be sure to immediately return them back to their tank. This is where the extra hides and the care and attention you have taken to create a safe and secure environment will come in handy. Your snake just needs time to calm down and adjust to their new environment, so it may be that you started handling them before they were ready. Returning them to their home and just allowing them to relax for a few days without any other interruptions should ensure that you maintain a calm and friendly snake.

Corn snakes are extremely resilient and will get over instances of trauma or discomfort very quickly, but that doesn't mean that they should be exposed to it again. If you have found that a particular way of handling the snake or picking them up has caused them to get anxious or upset, be sure to not repeat that gesture.

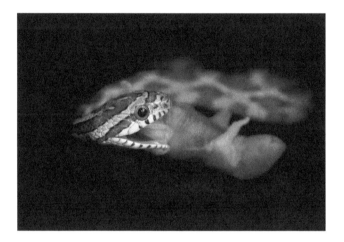

FEEDING

When it comes to feeding your snake for the first time, it's advisable to delay this until at least a week after you bring them home. They have a lot of exploring to do at that time and you want to make sure that when you feed them for the first time, they are hungry enough to eat straight away. In the next chapter, I will go much more in-depth as to what is involved in feeding and what you should be aware of. For now, though, it is enough to at least be prepared and ready for the first feeding and to know that your snake should not be given any food for the first 5 to 7 days.

When you purchase your corn snake, it is very important to ask if they have previously been fed any live mice or rodents. Most of the time, the answer will be no, as most pet shops and breeders generally start out by feeding frozen rodents and pinkies to the snakes and this is what you should also continue to do. But the reason you need to double-check this is all part of the process of ensuring the snake adapts to their new surroundings. If they have been given live rodents or if you found your snake in the wild, the first meal you will give them should actually be a live rodent. This is to try and keep some normality to their routine while they adjust. Then, once they know you and are comfortable in their new surroundings, you can start to change them to frozen rodents if you prefer.

If a snake has been raised in captivity and only fed frozen rodents, it is vitally important that you don't feed them a live mouse. This is because the snake won't be used to attacking prey and, if they don't manage the attack properly, the mouse could actually injure the snake as it tries to escape from its grasp. If you are feeding your snake a live rodent, for this reason, you must stay in the room until your snake has finished their meal.

CHAPTER SUMMARY

In this chapter, we have learned:

- What to keep in mind when bringing your corn snake home
- How to handle your corn snake and the most important things to remember before handling
- What you should feed your corn snake and how to manage this process
- Important facts to remember about handling and feeding with particular reference to the first week of bringing your snake home

IN THE NEXT CHAPTER, you will learn:

- Important factors to consider for the ongoing care of your corn snake

- What to feed your corn snake, how often and what is involved in the feeding process
- Key facts about the corn snake, how to handle them and what to expect from owning one as a pet
- How to make sure you are prepared for what is ahead as a responsible corn snake owner
- Important things to consider about the impact your new arrival may have on your home

CHAPTER FIVE: ONGOING CARE OF YOUR CORN SNAKE

There are some key time periods in the life of a corn snake that require some extra attention to ensure you are properly attending to all of their needs. When feeding your corn snake, try and make sure you don't feed them more than once per week and avoid all handling of the animal for a day or two after feeding.

If you prefer to start them off with a small live mouse that's fine, but it is preferable to move them to frozen mice as soon as possible. As well as being more convenient to feed them frozen rodents, it also reduces the chance that your snake might get injured. It is common for mice or rats to fight back if they are in a small cage with a snake that is about to eat them and this can inflict serious injury on your brand new pet. That is why it is advisable not to feed them straight away while the snake is disorientated by its new surroundings.

SHEDDING

Shedding is a natural part of your new pet's cycle and you should be aware of best practice and also how you can assist with making sure this is a stress-free process. Your corn snake will shed regularly when it is young, probably around every few weeks to start with, but as it grows to an adult size snake, this will become less frequent. Shedding is a crucial part of the growth process of your snake and it is also a good indicator of the general overall health of your pet. The shed should come off in one large piece, rather than in small flakes. If you find that your snake is instead shedding small pieces of skin, this usually points to a lack of humidity within the tank or availability of water. The corn snake will often coil up in the water bowl as part of the shedding process, so be particularly vigilant around this time that there is sufficient water and that it is being cleaned and replaced regularly.

The humid hide you have created in the tank will also provide a safe place for the snake to undertake the shedding process. Just before the snake starts to shed, you may notice the skin dulls slightly and the eyes will turn cloudy and bluish in color. When you start to notice these signs, that is your cue to make sure that the tank is humid with plenty of water and that the moss in the humid hide has been moistened. You may also wish to spray the tank with some lukewarm water mist from a spray bottle and you can even mist a light spray on your corn snake if they will let you. Do not do this if it agitates your snake and instead just focus on ensuring the environment is optimum for the shed to begin.

Moisture, Humidity And Shedding

Humidity levels in the cage should normally be between 35% and 50%, but for the duration of the shed, you should increase this to between 60% and 70%. Also, remember when designing your tank to include lots of coarse materials, like bark and wood, so that your snake can rub against them to aid with the shed. If you notice your corn snake is rubbing their nose against the coarse material, that is a sign that they are starting to try and shed.

At times you may find that your corn snake is having difficulty shedding its skin. In situations like this, you can help the process by soaking some paper towels in lukewarm water and holding your snake between several layers of these. The combination of your corn snake making its way through the towels and you gently maneuvering the towels will usually work in assisting with the removal of the skin. For continued issues with this, or if this solution doesn't work, always consult with your vet.

Once your corn snake has shed, you will need to clean the cage, being sure to remove all of the old shed for the maximum comfort of your pet. Remember that much like most of the processes in your corn snake's life - shedding can serve as a great indicator of the overall health of your pet. Anything that causes your animal stress or unnecessary suffering will also affect the shed, so please make sure you pay extra attention to your animal around this time.

CHAPTER SUMMARY

In this chapter, we have learned:

- Important factors to consider for the ongoing care of your corn snake
- What to feed your corn snake, how often and what is involved in the feeding process
- Key facts about the corn snake, how to handle them and what to expect from owning one as a pet
- How to make sure you are prepared for what is ahead as a responsible corn snake owner
- Important things to consider about the impact your new arrival may have on your home

IN THE NEXT CHAPTER, you will learn:

- Where to continue your journey as a corn snake enthusiast and how to find information in your local area
- How to find relevant information online, join community forums and expand your knowledge
- Further details about how to become a breeder of corn snakes and what you should be considering in advance of this
- More information about the species itself and how it fits in with other snake and reptile breeds

CHAPTER SIX: BECOMING A CORN SNAKE ENTHUSIAST

There are many dedicated reptile enthusiasts and it is very easy to find a whole host of information online that will provide you with support, guidance and best practice tips. YouTube, in particular, has a lot of great advisory channels and you can connect with most pet shops and reptile experts through their websites also. Corn snakes, in particular, are very popular with snake enthusiasts due to their qualities that make them fantastic pets.

Another type of event that has become common in recent years is pet expos, more specifically, reptile expos. These are conferences held in large cities where suppliers, experts, enthusiasts, breeders and community influencers come together for a few days of information sessions and events. These are great places to meet other reptile enthusiasts and you will also be able to pick up some great deals from local suppliers, as well as getting some key questions about the care and upkeep of your corn snake answered.

As with any pet, being a dedicated corn snake owner will mean you not only love talking about and researching your pet, but also enjoy interacting with other people and learning about new breeds. You might even decide that you want to share your own journey of becoming a new pet owner with other people and decide to set up your own YouTube channel to help other people with the early stages of being a new snake owner.

PET EXPOS

MAKE sure you ask several questions about the animal you are going to buy. This book provides general information about corn snakes, but your corn snake's temperament, diet and health may vary slightly depending on the breeder.

SUPPLIERS

YOU ALSO MAY BE able to buy a corn snake from a reptile expo. Breeders often go to expos to show off and sell their reptiles. Here's a list of well-known reptile expos in the United States. Check their websites to find out when they will be coming to your state.

- Repticon
- NARBC
- Reptidae

ALWAYS MAKE sure you get your corn snake from a reputable supplier. Try to get your corn snake from a trusted reptile breeder who has been breeding and selling snakes for a while. Do not get your snake from an amateur breeder. Be sure to inspect the snake and make sure it doesn't have any health defects. Do not buy a snake if the breeder will not allow you to handle the snake. Do not buy the snake if what the breeder is saying about the snake doesn't mesh with what you know about the breed of snake you want to buy. For example, if the breeder is trying to pass a milk snake off as a coral snake, this may be a sign that the breeder is not familiar with these animals and you need to look elsewhere.

DO NOT BUY **A Wild-Caught Snake**

ASK SPECIFICALLY FOR CAPTIVE-BRED SNAKES. If you opt to buy a wild-caught snake, you're more likely to get a nervous snake that will not trust you. This means you're more likely to get bitten when trying to handle it and that may encourage you not to handle it. It is possible to tame a wild-caught snake through proper handling, though.

ANOTHER GOOD REASON TO not get a wild-caught snake is that the seller may be selling them illegally or may be unwittingly hurting the local ecosystem by harvesting them from the wild. If this is practiced frequently, the niche that the corn snakes hold in the local ecosystem could be given to other predators or prey animals and the number of nuisance animals may increase because of it.

WILD SNAKES

DON'T BUY a wild-caught snake if anything seems off. If you aren't familiar with how to tell a venomous species from a non-venomous species, do not just take the breeder's word for it if you suspect that they are wild-caught snakes or that the breeder isn't knowledgeable.

ALTHOUGH THEY COME in different morphs, corn snakes have a certain look to them. If your snake does not have this look to it, there's a chance that it's not a corn snake. You should probably not buy that snake but instead, look for another breeder.

LEARN **About Your Snake's Diett**

SOME SNAKES ARE VERY picky eaters and will not transition easily from what they were eating before to whatever you decide to feed them. That means that if your snake was being fed live rodents before, you may have a very hard time getting it to accept frozen feeder mice. Putting up with the inconvenience of having to feed a snake live mice, however, is much better than having to deal with a snake that refuses to eat.

IF YOU DO GET a snake that refuses to eat, try other varieties of food. For example, if it won't accept frozen rodents, try live ones. A snake that refuses to eat for several days may need to visit a vet or an experienced herpetologist to get to the bottom of the issue.

REMEMBER **- When Choosing A Snake**

- Watch out for health problems

- Snakes can develop neurological issues from an improper diet
- Check it for ticks and mites
- Always ask to handle the snake before you buy it. If the breeder or supplier will not allow you to touch the snake, do not buy it

CHAPTER SUMMARY

In this chapter, we have learned:

- Where to continue your journey as a corn snake enthusiast and how to find information in your local area
- How to find relevant information online and join in with community forums and expand your knowledge
- Further details about how to become a breeder of corn snakes and what you should be considering in advance of this
- More information about the species itself and how it fits in with other snake and reptile breeds

IN THE NEXT CHAPTER, you will learn:

- Important points about the health and wellbeing of your corn snake
- How to identify certain health problems
- How to choose a good vet
- How to look for snake health insurance

CHAPTER SEVEN: HEALTH AND WELLBEING

orn Snake Health

Corn snakes are actually pretty hardy animals, meaning that they don't easily get sick and can withstand minor problems or changes in the environment that could kill other species of snake. That said, there are things you need to watch out for with your new pet.

Don't Let Your Snake Get Too Cold

Remember that snakes are animals that we refer to as ectothermic or "cold-blooded", meaning they cannot regulate their body temperatures sufficiently just using their bodies. Instead, they regulate their body temperatures using their environment.

Without basking in the sun or lying on warm ground in the wild, snakes would have a difficult time maintaining the proper body temperature for vital processes and would likely die. The disadvantage your pet snake has, however, is that its enclosure isn't a lot of room to explore and it can easily become too cold if the temperature isn't monitored closely.

Provide Warm Bedding

Make sure to provide warm substrate, also sometimes called bedding, such as leaf litter, aspen shavings, or cypress mulch for your snake to burrow under and keep itself warm. Also make sure to clean the cage and change the material regularly if your setup requires this. Alternatively, you can also use a substrate that a snake may find in its natural environment, especially if you are setting up a vivarium where part of the snake's enclosure replicates the conditions of its natural habitat. If you are not sure what kind of substrate to choose when setting up a tank with conditions that mimic the snake's natural environment, reach out to other snake enthusiasts or consult a knowledgeable breeder or pet shop. Just be sure that whatever you choose will absorb moisture, provide a warm place for your snake to burrow and be fairly easy to clean.

It is beneficial to you and your new pet if you do the proper work and research to set up your vivarium so that conditions in the snake's enclosure closely replicate what the snake would have in its natural environment in regards to temperature, complementary organisms and substrate. This can cut down on certain maintenance tasks and, in some cases, eliminate the need to do certain cleaning and maintenance tasks completely.

Don't Let Your Snake Get Too Hot

Your snake's enclosure should be kept at around 78 to 80 degrees Fahrenheit, or about 25 to 27 degrees Celsius, with a heat source that reaches up to 80 or 85 degrees Fahrenheit, or about 27 to 30 degrees Celsius. The warm side of the enclosure should take up no more than one-third of your snake's enclosure. You should not allow the warm side in your snake's enclosure to exceed 90 degrees Fahrenheit. However, wild corn snakes do live in environments that reach these temperatures and they may be okay as long as you provide sufficient opportunities for them to cool themselves off, such as a water bath where they can dip themselves and regulate their temperatures.

Also, make sure that one side of the snake's enclosure remains around 75 degrees Fahrenheit. Your snake will need a chance to cool itself off and it may get sick or injured if it just stays in the water. Too much moisture for a prolonged period of time can lead to conditions such as scale rot, a bacterial infection that could be harmful to your snake if it doesn't get proper treatment. If you live in a climate that naturally maintains high hot temperatures, you may have to do more work cooling your snake's environment than heating it. A bowl of cool, not cold, water, humid hide, and ample hiding spots away from the warm side of the enclosure should be sufficient.

You may also need a special heating pad designed for reptile enclosures. Do not use one designed for other purposes, as it may be easily damaged or become too hot and pose a potential health risk to you and your pet. In the wild during the day, a corn snake's natural habitat may reach up to 90 degrees, but when using an artificial heat source, it's best to turn it to a lower setting, around 80-85 degrees, to prevent overheating.

Direct Sunlight

Avoid exposing your corn snake to direct sunlight. This is a very easy way to overheat your snake without even realizing it. A glass or plastic reptile enclosure can retain far more heat than is recommended. Think about leaving a child or pet in a car with the windows up. That can happen to your snake if you leave the enclosure in a place that receives direct sunlight. Just don't do it.

Heating Lamps

Heating lamps are ideal for species of snakes that like to bask in the sun in the wild. Corn snakes prefer to receive their heat from the ground, not from basking in the sun, so heat lamps are not the best way to help your corn snake regulate its body temperature. When not used properly, they can actually injure or overheat your corn snake by making the enclosure too warm.

Heating Pads That Are Not Monitored

An under-the-tank reptile heating pad is the right tool to help your snake regulate its temperature, but you have to make sure you've installed it correctly. Incorrectly installing a heating mat can result in damage to your enclosure, injury to your animal and potential safety issues in the form of fire risks.

First of all, make sure that your tank is sitting off of the ground. The heating pad or mat should not come in direct contact with the enclosure. The mat should come with something to help you elevate the enclosure, like pegs you can place underneath to ensure that the glass or plastic enclosure sits slightly above the heat source. You should make sure that the mat does not touch the bottom of the tank. Having the mat in direct contact with the glass or plastic surface can trap heat and make it warmer than it should be, causing damage to the enclosure or heat mat and potentially hurting your animal. It could also pose a fire risk.

It is also recommended that you place a piece of tin foil over the adhesive side of the mat to prevent it from touching the enclosure directly and so that you can re-use your heat mat with multiple enclosures. The adhesive side on some heating mats is too sticky to successfully remove the heating pad after placing it directly onto a glass or plastic surface without damaging the heating pad. Plus, you don't want it directly touching the glass or plastic bottom of the enclosure anyway, because there's a chance it will get much too hot. There are some mats, however, that can be placed directly on the outside of the enclosure on a low setting. It's still recommended, however, that you don't use a heat mat directly on the outside of the enclosure, especially if you don't know how hot the heat mat itself is. The mat will always be hotter than the temperature inside the cage.

More Information

Do not place the temperature gauge or any of the measurement equipment directly on top of the heat mat. Instead, place the gauge inside of the tank and place the probes in an area where they can accurately measure the temperature of the warm spot. Placing the temperature measurement equipment directly on the heat mat will produce readings that are deceptively high and may lead you to believe that the temperature inside of your enclosure is much too warm for your pet, even though it may be in fact at a reasonable temperature. The temperature measurement equipment is meant to be placed inside the tank, not on the heating mat. Don't cause yourself the frustration and risk of burning or freezing your pet due to this much too common tank setup error.

Never place the heating mat inside of the tank. It lacks the waterproofing necessary to withstand the conditions the tank may experience, such as if the snake spills its water or excretes waste in the area where the heating mat is placed. Exposing the mat to too much moisture could damage it, present a fire hazard and create a potentially dangerous situation for you and your pet.

Do not use the mat inside of the enclosure and remember to follow all included instructions before placing the heating mat. If the instructions you read on the package or instruction manual seem to contradict information you've read or heard elsewhere, consult the opinion of a seasoned snake owner or pet shop. There's a good chance you may be misinterpreting what you've read and it's a bad idea to try to set up a new environment if you are not fairly sure of what you are supposed to be doing. There's also a chance you've purchased the wrong product. If anything seems off, consult the expertise of a more experienced corn snake owner to find out if you have the right product. The wrong thing could damage your enclosure and injure your snake.

HEATING ROCKS

THESE ITEMS ARE PLACED within the tank to provide the snake with a source of heat. The problem is they often get too hot, increasing the likelihood that your snake will burn itself. Do not use a heating rock, unless your enclosure setup necessitates it. An example of when you might need to use a source of heat placed inside of the cage with corn snakes is if you're keeping the snake in an enclosure with a wooden bottom. Wood is too thick for heat from the heating mat to penetrate sufficiently to warm it without creating a fire hazard. In a situation where the tank bottom is wooden or covered by wood, you might decide to use a heating source that is meant to be placed inside of the cage. This way, the snake can get warm even though a heating mat at the bottom of the cage would not work.

IF YOU DO FIND yourself in a situation where you have to use a heat source that is placed inside of the cage, monitor it carefully. Place the temperature measuring probes directly on the heat source itself and make sure it gets no hotter than 85 degrees Fahrenheit or 30 degrees Celsius. A heat source over 85 degrees may potentially cause problems for your snake. If your in-cage heat source is hotter than 85 degrees, turn down the temperature. If you have no way of regulating the temperature with the equipment you currently have, you may have to purchase a compatible temperature regulation system. If you can't find a compatible system, your tank setup may not work. Don't risk injuring your new pet or exposing it to inade-quate living conditions. Instead, either look for an alternative setup or do not get a pet corn snake.

ALWAYS HAVE **A Method Of Measuring The Temperature In The Tank**

YOU SHOULD ALWAYS HAVE a method of measuring and regulating the temperature in the enclosure. If the enclosure gets too hot, your snake could die or experience serious health problems. Most people use a thermometer with a probe to measure the temperature. As described above, you should place the thermometer inside the enclosure. If you feel like you need to further regulate the temperature, you can use a thermostat. Connect the thermostat to the heating pad by plugging the heating pad's power cord into the body of the reptile heating pad thermostat. Make sure that the heater you choose is compatible with having a thermostat attached to it.

DIFFERENT KINDS **Of Enclosures**

Glass

GLASS ENCLOSURES HAVE a few advantages over plastic ones. They can be exposed to more direct heat without the threat of melting and they hold less overall humidity. If you have a glass enclosure, you can stick your heating pad or heating mat directly to the enclosure, although this is not always recommended. Likewise, if your snake requires a basking lamp, you can hang it directly over the snake's basking area without worrying about melting or burning anything.

Plastic

PLASTIC ENCLOSURES ARE INEXPENSIVE, but they are not as durable as glass enclosures. You may end up melting or burning the enclosure if you set up your heat source incorrectly. Be sure to get a thermostat and measure the temperature carefully. Don't let your heat source exceed 90 degrees and don't put it directly on the plastic container.

WOOD

AS MENTIONED ABOVE, if you have a custom-built enclosure made of wood, steel or aluminum, you may need to try another heat source besides a heat mat because wood may not transfer enough heat to the inside of the snake's enclosure. You may want to try a heat rock or other in-cage heating source. Find one that is compatible with a thermostat. Remember to place the thermostat probe directly on the heat source and keep the heat source around 85-90 degrees, no warmer. If you have a custom-built enclosure, though, you may be a more experienced snake keeper and you may already know how to properly warm your snake.

WHY YOU NEED **To Keep Your Snake Warm**

CORN SNAKES NEED to warm to a certain body temperature to aid their digestion and other body processes. Recall that snakes are ectothermic and, as such, they do a poor job of regulating their own body temperature without help. Snakes that are too cold slow down and may suffer poor health if they are kept at too low a temperature for too long. Corn snakes prefer to get their heat from the ground and do not prefer to come out and bask, so sources of ground heat are ideal for the snake.

WHAT SHOULD you do if your snake gets too warm? If the heat source gets the heating area too hot, the snake may burn itself. If your snake burns itself, immediately remove the heat source from the enclosure. Check the temperature of the warm side. If it's over 90 degrees, it is too hot. Remove your snake and place it in a cooler enclosure to keep the burn from getting worse.

IMMEDIATELY CONTACT your vet if it looks like your snake has a visible scar or welt from where it was burned. It may need immediate treatment to stabilize its condition and prevent the burn site from becoming infected. Follow up your vet visit by bathing the snake in betadine or over-the-counter snake soak meant for burn treatment. Dry the snake off and place it in an enclosure where the warm side is around 85-90 degrees. Be sure to constantly measure the temperature of the warm spot by placing the thermostat's probe on the floor of the enclosure where the heat source is radiating. If the probe reads that it is higher than 90 degrees, it is too hot. Turn down the temperature using the thermostat controls and keep the snake away from the heat source. If the warm spot continues to get too hot, even with a thermostat placed on it, remove the heat source and look for another one. The heat source may be defective. Exposing the snake to too warm a temperature for too long may cause the snake to overheat and die. You may also risk burning the snake again or aggravating the burn site.

HOW TO PREVENT **Burns**

TEST YOUR HEATING source and vivarium equipment before you bring your snake home. Make sure that the thermometer and any associated probes are reading the temperature accurately. Remember to place the thermometer inside of the enclosure, not directly on the heat source! If the temperature in the warm spot fluctuates past 90 degrees Fahrenheit, get a thermostat. Do not introduce your corn snake to the enclosure until you verify that the heating mechanism is heating the warm spot to no more than 90 degrees Fahrenheit. Also make sure that the snake isn't exposed to other sources of burns, like hot lights or exposed basking lamps. Corn snakes don't need basking lamps and too many heat sources will just make the enclosure too hot and may harm your pets. Once you've introduced your corn snake to the environment, check the temperature frequently to make sure the thermostat is functioning correctly. Make sure that the temperature in the warm spot remains 90 degrees Fahrenheit or a little below, never above.

DON'T LET **Your Corn Snake Sit In Damp Conditions**

EXPOSING your snake to too much humidity or leaving it in damp dirty conditions could lead to an infection called scale rot. Scale rot is a bacterial infection of the skin from being exposed to overly moist or unsanitary conditions. Signs of scale rot include reddish-brown ulcerations and erosion of the scales with large blisters on the belly. If left untreated, scale rot can be fatal.

HOW TO TREAT **Scale Rot**

CONSULT your vet right away if you believe your snake is suffering from scale rot. The vet may prescribe special antibiotics to help your snake, but that's not all you need to do to make sure your snake has a healthy recovery. Start by lowering the humidity in the tank. Clean and dry the enclosure thoroughly. Replace the substrate with aspen bedding and test the humidity levels inside of the cage using a hygrometer. Your corn snake does not need to be in an environment with high humidity. Keep the humidity levels between 40 and 50 percent. If the humidity is still too high, move the watering bowl to the cool side of the tank and test the humidity levels in the room. If the humidity in the room is too high, seal off the room and get a dehumidifier. If you catch it early, you can use an antibiotic ointment to treat your snake.

OTHER HEALTH PROBLEMS

Paramyxovirus

THIS IS a pathogen that causes mainly respiratory symptoms and it is highly contagious. A snake with this virus may "stargaze", gaping while looking up at its enclosure with dilated pupils. This may be a sign that it is having trouble breathing. If you see your snake doing this, please contact your vet immediately. If your snake develops tremors, convulsions, or other neurological problems, it might be too late. It is likely your snake will die of this virus if the symptoms that are preventing it from breathing are not addressed.

PREVENTION

THERE IS no known vaccine to prevent this virus. It is sometimes found in wild species of snakes. To decrease your risk of bringing it into your home and infecting pet snakes, do not catch wild snakes or handle snakes taken from the wild. If you suspect you may have a snake with the virus, quarantine it and contact your veterinarian. Be sure to thoroughly clean and sterilize your hands after handling snakes that may be infected. This disease is often seen in vipers, but other snakes can be infected with it, too.

NEUROLOGICAL PROBLEMS

ONE NEUROLOGICAL ISSUE snakes can develop is caused by a thiamin deficiency. This deficiency is caused by feeding snakes certain kinds of fish and by not providing vitamin supplements to snakes on a fish diet. Corn snakes should not be fed anything but rodents, so this should not be an issue with your snake. If you suspect your snake is acting odd, though, or if you see symptoms of neurological problems, it might have a vitamin deficiency. Feed the snake food dusted in a snake vitamin powder, if available. Before further treating the snake, take your animal to a vet to determine the cause of the issue.

OTHER PROBLEMS **your snake may develop:**

- Mites - your vet may recommend a special medicated bath or spray made especially for reptiles
- Breathing problems - take it to the vet, as it might be a sign of a more serious issue
- Skin problems - take it to the vet
- Serious injuries - take it to a vet
- Lethargy - your snake may be too cold. Make sure the temperature of the enclosure isn't below 75 degrees Fahrenheit. If that doesn't work, take it to the vet

CHOOSING A VET

WHEN CHOOSING a veterinarian for your corn snake, don't go with a run-of-the-mill general practitioner, if you can help it. Look for someone who specializes in treating reptiles or even specializes in snakes if you can find anyone in your area. A general practitioner, who treats all small animals may not have the expertise necessary to care for special reptilian problems. After all, reptiles are much different than mammals and birds and snakes are different than some reptiles. It's best to find an experienced veterinarian who can quickly identify common problems without having to run lots of expensive tests. If you select a vet that relies only on what their tests and instruments tell them, you may end up spending a lot caring for your pet.

UNFORTUNATELY, health insurance for pets isn't as easy to come by as it is for humans, so you may end up discouraged from going to the vet if your pet gets sick if you select a vet that runs itself like a human hospital. They may provide the best care if you can afford it, but you may be looking at thousands of dollars in tests just to find out what's wrong. It's better to have a doctor who doesn't have to run tests to find out and treat common ailments because it helps you save money and doesn't discourage you from taking your animal to the vet if something is really wrong.

WHEN CHOOSING a veterinarian for your corn snake, look for someone who has extensive experience working with and treating reptiles. If you can, find a vet that is very experienced and has been working for many years. An experienced veterinarian will have seen a lot of different reptiles and a lot of different reptile problems and will be better able to quickly diagnose your pet.

PET INSURANCE

PET INSURANCE MAY BE available for your snake, although most companies only insure dogs and cats. One or more companies, such as Nationwide, may also insure small animals, such as rabbits and snakes. Depending on when you are reading this book, insurance coverage for small animals may still be available. It may be helpful to do a quick internet search to find out what providers are available in your area and what kinds of pet care they cover. A knowledgeable veterinarian may be able to give you more information and even help you apply for coverage. If insurance is available, please consider applying for it. It may drastically cut down the amount you have to spend on your animal's healthcare bills and make vet visits less stressful for you.

CHAPTER SUMMARY

IN THIS CHAPTER, we have learned:

- Common diseases that can afflict corn snakes and how to identify them
- How to prepare your snake for a vet visit
- When you should take the snake to the vet
- How to find the best vet for your snake

IN THE NEXT CHAPTER, you will learn:

- Some important points to keep in mind about licensing and permitting and how to find out if corn snakes are allowed where you live

CHAPTER EIGHT: LICENSING AND PREFERRED SUPPLIERS

Once you have decided that a corn snake is the right pet for you, it is important to make sure you are fully familiar with all the legalities, licensing restrictions, animal health and any vaccination or insurance requirements. These will depend very much on the area in which you live but, outlined below, you will find some of the main points you should consider and where you can find further information specific to your location.

Licensing

Laws regarding corn snake ownership can be a bit convoluted because the corn snake is actually a native species in certain parts of the United States. Some states prohibit the sale of animals that are native to the region in an effort to prevent animals from being harvested from the wild. This doesn't necessarily mean that you can't legally own a corn snake in the states where sale and ownership of native species are usually prohibited, however. In fact, in many cases, you are allowed to own these animals without a permit, even in states where they are considered a native species. Unfortunately, like with everything else, there are exceptions. Some states have laws on the books that would make corn snake ownership illegal and there is always a strong possibility of laws being changed or revised to suit what is considered best for the wildlife and the ecosystems in those states.

Plus, what is legal this year is not guaranteed to be legal next year and what was illegal this year isn't guaranteed to remain illegal, as populations of wild native species recover from being illegally hunted, eaten, or outcompeted by opportunistic invasive predators. Still, though, it's best to play it safe and carefully research your state's individual ownership laws. This also applies to you if you are outside of the United States. Your country, province, or region may have laws against the ownership of certain animals or may require you to have a permit or a special license to keep them. It's important to do the research and ask the right questions because if you don't, your harmless journey to corn snake ownership may turn out to be expensive and inconvenient.

Why Such Laws Exist

You may ask yourself, why does such a law even exist in the first place? After all, they aren't poisonous and they don't grow large enough to eat anyone. They also don't pose a risk to local wildlife when cared for properly. The key here is "when cared for properly". You may be an extremely responsible reptile owner, but the government doesn't know that. They're aware, however, of when exotic animal ownership didn't go so smoothly, either for the owners, for the environment, or for the unfortunate people who found potentially dangerous neglected exotic pets.

Let's take what happened in Florida, for example. Reports of reticulated pythons that were abandoned by their owners attacking children, pets and wildlife started showing up in the news. In response to these disasters and woeful examples of animal neglect, legislation was passed in Florida against ownership of certain non-indigenous snake species. These abandoned pets were breeding in the wild and had become a dangerous invasive species that was destroying Florida's native wildlife and harming ecosystems. The problem got so bad that it was proposed that certain kinds of snakes be added to the Lacey Act, to prevent what happened in Florida from happening in other states.

In the United States, ownership of certain snakes, such as venomous snakes and large constrictors, is regulated. To keep such a snake as a pet or for other purposes, the owner is required to purchase a permit and sometimes undergo an inspection to ensure the owner has the proper enclosures to keep the snakes safely and ensure they don't escape and hurt other people or wildlife. These laws and regulations are intended to keep the snakes from harming humans and native wildlife, as there have been many cases in the past where a negligent pet owner has released a pet snake into the wild and it has harmed local ecosystems by out-competing native wildlife for food sources or in some cases destroying native wildlife populations by making them into prey items. In other cases, the snakes have even posed a threat to the lives of adults and young children. No one wants to have uninvited cobras, black mambas, or anacondas living in their backyards and making the area potentially unsafe. Those snakes can be deadly under the right conditions. Certain species are regulated in an effort to prevent this and, considering the risk some exotic species pose, this measure is fairly lenient.

THE LACEY ACT

This is an act in the United States that prevents certain animals from being part of interstate trade. The intent is to keep them from finding habitats in the United States, breeding and becoming an invasive species. There has been controversy about the addition of certain snake species to this act because advocates argue that it unfairly punishes responsible reptile owners. Opponents of this act may make some good points. Did you know that it may be illegal under this act to take your exotic pet to another state for vet treatment, for example? Some think that this act is unnecessarily harsh and extreme.

THERE ARE NO LICENSING REQUIREMENTS, however, to keep a pet corn snake in many parts of the United States. In some parts of the US, they're considered an exotic species and only native species are regulated unless they pose a potential threat to humans. Corn snakes are non-venomous and are too small to be harmful to humans, so they do not fit into the category of regulated snakes. That doesn't necessarily mean, however, that you will be allowed to keep a pet corn snake where you live. If you live in a warmer part of the US, you may not be allowed to keep a corn snake for another reason - the state wants to prevent people from gathering them from the wild. Sometimes states place bans on owning any animal that is considered a native species and can be collected from the wild. This is intended to prevent people from collecting native animals and selling them across state borders, as collecting native animals and selling them can again hurt the fragile ecosystem.

LICENSING AND PERMITS

INSTEAD OF AN OUTRIGHT BAN, locations that are having problems with abandoned pets could consider enacting legislation that requires the owners of certain snake species to have a special license or permit to keep the animals.

States That Ban Corn Snake Ownership

The information presented here may or may not be accurate, depending on when you're reading this book. Laws change depending on what populations want and if native wildlife populations recover or new laws get passed, these bans can be lifted and requirements can be changed.

Georgia

In the state of Georgia, corn snakes are considered a native species and breeding them for sale is illegal. You may, however, be allowed to obtain a permit to keep them for educational display. It actually may be easier to own a venomous snake in the state of Georgia due to the permit requirements.

Tennessee

In Tennessee, corn snakes are also considered a native species and are not allowed to be kept as pets and bred without a permit. Again, you may be allowed to keep them for educational display if you are willing to undergo the required inspections. There may be other states that have complete and partial bans, as well as other potential bans in the works. Sometimes bans come about from real concern for the environment. Other times, they are created due to false or incomplete information or to solve temporary local problems.

How You Can Influence Snake Ownership Laws

If you want to have a voice regarding whether or not you are allowed to own corn snakes in your area, you may want to get involved with the reptile ownership advocacy groups in your country. Without knowing all sides of the debate, lawmakers are more likely to take ban requests seriously, even if they have no basis in reality. Luckily for some fans of exotic reptiles, reptile advocacy groups are politically active and willing to lobby for pet reptile enthusiasts. You can help by adding your voice to petitions, writing letters to your state legislators and finding enthusiast groups in your area. Bans due to safety concerns usually come from misinformation and mishandling. Sometimes people lobby for bans due to experiences they've had due to mishandling or mistreating the animals or experiences with the animals related to them being mistreated. If you don't think other people should be punished for the mistakes of a few, join with the politically active enthusiast groups in your area.

States Where You Can Own A Corn Snake Without A Permit

- Alabama
- Alaska
- Arizona
- Arkansas

There are other states that allow corn snakes that do not appear on this list. For more information about corn snakes and states that allow you to own them, check out the Library of Congress website. You can also check out the individual state government websites.

It's also important to note that state requirements are often very different from local ordinances. Whereas the state may say that it is okay for you to own a certain animal, your local city ordinances may say otherwise. For example, you will probably not be allowed to raise hens or other livestock animals in certain areas, even though they are approved for private ownership in your state.

Even if corn snakes are allowed in your city, they may not be allowed in your individual neighborhood or building. If you live in a snake or reptile-free neighborhood, you may incur fines if you try to own one, even if you are legally allowed to own a corn snake in your state and city and even if you have the right permits to do so. Different areas have different sensitivities and home-owners associations or HOAs and apartment complexes have the right to restrict pet ownership.

CHAPTER SUMMARY

IN THIS CHAPTER, we have learned:

- About licensing and restrictions
- Why a corn snake owner may be required to have a license
- Why corn snake ownership is banned in some states
- Why you might want to join a reptile owner advocacy group

IN THE NEXT CHAPTER, you will learn:

- About the training and conditioning of snakes

CHAPTER NINE: TRAINING AND BEHAVIOR MODIFICATION

T raining And Behavior Modification

FIRST OF ALL, snakes are reptiles and reptiles cannot be trained in the traditional sense. If you are expecting to be able to train your pet like a cat or a dog, you may be extremely disappointed. Reptiles lack the intelligence to be able to register things like emotion or semi-complex reasoning that mammals sometimes engage in. Show a rat how to solve a complex puzzle to receive a reward, and the rat will learn how to solve the puzzle, eventually with very little input from its handler. It will also be able to carry over some of what it learned previously to other puzzles it's presented with. With reptiles, unfortunately, this is not the case. Their ability to think and reason is much more primitive and instinct-driven. Reptile behavior, however, can be modified slightly through a process known as conditioning.

WHAT IS CONDITIONING?

CONDITIONING IS a behavior modification process that involves reinforcing a certain response with the intention of making it more frequent. For example, if you want to teach your dog to fetch and you notice that the dog already brings you items in its mouth, you would feed the dog a treat every time it comes to you with an item in its mouth to ensure that it keeps up this behavior. Eventually, the dog would learn that if it carries items to you in its mouth, it will receive a treat.

CLASSICAL CONDITIONING

WITH MORE INTELLIGENT MAMMALS, you can use conditioning to train them to distinguish different words that you say and gestures that you make and you can teach them to perform complex patterns of behavior on command. Dogs are an excellent example of this. These particular mammals are so trainable that they can be trusted with "jobs" in our society and we've all heard of search and rescue dogs, fire dogs, drug-sniffing dogs and seeing-eye dogs. Horses and pigs have a similar level of intelligence to dogs and can even do some of the things dogs are traditionally trained to do, such as search for specific items or guide the blind. Don't be surprised if you run into a seeing-eye horse or a truffle sniffing pig, as these animals are well equipped to perform these duties. Even cats and mice can be trained to perform complex tricks, such as playing the piano or ringing a bell on command to please audiences, by way of more complex conditioning. These simple tricks can be put to other uses as well, such as having a cat wear a camera or a mouse lie still during an injection.

WHAT ABOUT REPTILES?

LESS INTELLIGENT ANIMALS, like reptiles, may only be able to learn simple cause and effect associations. For example, lizards can be taught to recognize and move toward colored targets. These are used to help move them if their areas need to be cleaned, if they need medicine, or if they are in any danger. Like all animals, reptiles will learn to associate cause with effect. If the target is presented and the lizard walks toward it, the lizard will be fed. The lizard will, therefore, learn to walk toward the target to get fed - this is simple cause and effect.

WHY THIS IS **Important**

LET'S say that you often put your hand in your snake's cage when it is time for you to feed the snake. This causes the snake to associate your hand in its cage with food being presented and may promote biting the next time you try to handle it. In this scenario, you accidentally conditioned your snake to associate your hand with food and you may end up with more aggressive behavior from your pet the next time you try to handle it or take it out to clean its cage.

HOW TO CORRECT **This**

PRESENT your clean hand to the snake when you are not feeding it and let it get used to your feel and smell. Gradually touch the snake to let it know that you are not a threat. Practice handling your snake on a regular basis to help it become comfortable with your presence and not show aggressive behavior. Creating a routine will help your snake distinguish whether or not you are feeding it and it may reduce biting and other kinds of aggressive behavior by cutting down on its stress. If your snake does not know what to expect, it may feel threatened and try to defend itself.

RESPECT your pet by giving it space and letting it adjust to routines gradually. Be consistent with the routines you establish. If you decide that you will touch the snake lightly to let it know that you intend to handle it, keep up the habit. Don't decide one day that you will try to pick it up without warning because that may elicit a biting response.

ALTERNATIVELY, you can try feeding the snake with special feeding tongs so that it does not begin to associate the smell of your hand with food in the first place. You can also try feeding it in a different location than in its cage, so it does not associate opening its cage with the possibility of being fed.

CHAPTER SUMMARY

IN THIS CHAPTER, we have learned:

- It is possible to condition most animals, including reptiles.
- Reptiles may not be as trainable as birds or mammels
- You can use conditioning and other behavior modification techniques on snakes

IN THE NEXT CHAPTER, you will learn:

- Some helpful information pertaining to breeding your snakes.

CHAPTER TEN: BREEDING

B
reeding And Caring For Baby Snakes

Sexing snakes

There are three ways to attempt to identify the sex of a snake. One is by sight. The other two involve techniques that are somewhat physically invasive. Only sight identification techniques are safe to do if you are not trained. Done correctly, using physical means to properly identify what sex your snake is will not hurt it. However, it is not recommended that you try to do physically invasive techniques without special training. Doing so could seriously injure your pet, making it unfit for breeding and injury can cause pain, infection and even death.

Common Traits Used For Sight Identification

Look at the width of your snake's tail

Male snakes can sometimes be identified by their broader, wider tail where they store their male reproductive organs. This means that the tail after the cloaca will remain just as thick and taper off closer to the tip of the tail. This method, however, isn't foolproof. A healthy muscular female can be misidentified as a male and a young scrawny male can be misidentified as a female.

Compare the size of your snake with other snakes.

Male corn snakes usually grow bigger than female corn snakes, but again, this isn't foolproof. You can have female corn snakes that are healthy and relatively large and you can also have scrawny adult male corn snakes.

Popping

One sure method of identifying your snake's sex, in many cases, is known as "popping". Using this method, you squeeze and roll the snake's genitalia until it "pops" out of the cloaca. This method allows you to see the genitalia and confirm for sure whether the snake is male or female.

Warning! This should only be attempted by someone who knows the technique! Again, if you have not been trained by a professional on how to do this procedure correctly, do not attempt it. Improper handling of a snake can cause it serious injury. It's easy to break a snake's spine by applying too much pressure and, if you do, you may end up having to have your snake humanely euthanized so that it will not continue to suffer pain. Don't be reckless. If you don't know what you're doing and are curious about your snake's gender, consult an expert for help. You may injure the snake by squeezing it too hard and breaking its small bones. Remember, do not attempt this without a trained professional or without receiving training to do it correctly first.

Once you've been correctly shown how to do this by a professional and you are confident you know what you are doing, you can safely do this at home. Hold the snake gently in a partial belly-up position and look for a flap on the bottom side of its tail. Place your thumb on the pocket of skin that hides the snake's cloaca and, with your other hand, gently roll and push the side closest to the tip of the tail. If you see hemipenes pop out, it's a male snake. Hemipenes are parts of the male reproductive organ of a snake and they work in a similar way to the penis of other animals, helping fertilize the eggs of the female. The hemipenes are usually held inverted until they are everted for reproduction or via mechanical or hormonal stimulation.

In addition to hemipenes, males also have sperm plugs that help ensure that the sperm deposited into the female is not expelled and also serves to keep other males from successfully mating with females who have already recently mated. If you don't see hemipenes, the snake may be female. There's also the possibility that you did not do the procedure correctly, unfortunately. If you suspect it might be the latter, try probing the snake instead.

Probing

Another method of identifying your snake's sex is called probing. This time, the procedure is to insert an instrument into the part of the cloaca where the genitals would be stored. It is important not to force the instrument in or apply too much pressure. Snakes are very delicate creatures and, as with the previous example, they can be injured easily through improper handling.

Warning! This should only be attempted by someone who knows the technique! Inserting a foreign instrument into the body of your pet should only be done by a trained professional, under the supervision of a trained professional, or after the one performing the procedure has undergone significant special training to ensure the procedure is done correctly. Incorrectly inserting the probe can cause the snake discomfort, injury, infection and may even lead to death. If you do puncture your snake, make sure you take it to a vet right away so that a trained professional can fix your mistake, either by neutering and patching up the animal or by humanely euthanizing it.

To prevent yourself from having to take your pet to the vet, though, and maybe enduring an expensive and otherwise unnecessary surgery to fix a botched sexing, just take your pet to the vet and have the veterinarian sex your pet during a routine checkup. You could also have it performed by any reputable reptile breeders or enthusiasts in your area. Professional snake breeders should be well acquainted with the process of sexing snakes and identifying if they are in the proper shape for breeding.

If you have been properly trained, you can proceed with this technique. To "probe" your snake, gently insert a special snake sexing probing tool into the flap that covers the cloaca and push it forward toward the tip of the tail. Do not push if you feel any resistance, as doing so may result in injuring the snake and puncturing important organs. Now, measure how far your probe went. If your probe went past six of your snake's scales, there's a good chance it's a male snake. If your probe only went down five scales or less, there's a chance it might be a female or an immature male. If you are not sure of the snake's age or if you have a young snake, measure it again when it gets older, or try using the popping technique. If you do this process correctly, your snake may experience minor discomfort. Done incorrectly, though, this process can be very painful and stressful for your snake. It is highly recommended that you consult a professional before attempting to sex a snake on your own. You may forget very important steps that ensure your snake remains healthy.

Remember to keep careful records of what gender your snakes are after you find out for sure. Sexing your snakes often might upset them or stress them out. Unlike mammals, reptiles, like snakes and lizards, keep their reproductive organs stored securely inside of their bodies and procedures to find out their sex are more or less invasive and potentially painful.

How To Tell If Your Snake Is Ready To Breed

Corn snakes are ready to breed at 18 to 24 months of age. To get them ready to breed, you may want to recreate slightly cooler conditions in their enclosure, around 55 degrees Fahrenheit, for a three month period to make them react the way they would when coming out of winter rest. Slowly warm the snakes up to simulate spring and feed them every 2 to 3 days. When the female is ready, put her into a breeding tank with the male. Remove the male after they mate. Once the female lays her eggs, remove the eggs and put them into an incubation tank.

CHAPTER SUMMARY

IN THIS CHAPTER, we have learned:

- How to sex snakes visually
- How to sex snakes physically
- How to prepare them for breeding

IN THE NEXT CHAPTER, you will learn:

- About rehoming and euthanasia

CHAPTER ELEVEN: REHOMING AND EUTHANASIA

You may not want to imagine this could ever happen to you, but circumstances do change and it may be a good idea to make sure you have a plan in place in case you can no longer care for your pet. This will prevent unnecessary hardship for you and will decrease the stress level and danger your pet may face if you are no longer able to care for it. If you cannot continue to take care of your snake for any reason, you need to consider rehoming it. Rehoming your snake ensures that it doesn't end up out in the wild where it can potentially breed and contribute to the invasive species problem. For states where corn snakes are a native species, it means that you won't be putting extra stress on your snake by forcing it to fend for itself and have a much harsher life than when you were taking care of it.

To properly rehome a snake, take it to a reptile enthusiast who will accept your abandoned reptile and give it a good home until someone else adopts it. You may have to shop around to find people in your area who house rescue reptiles. Usually, those who run rescues specialize in a certain kind of animal. Look for someone who special-izes in rescuing constrictors. Of course, there's a process to handing over your snake. It may involve some paperwork or it may involve having to hand your snake over in person. Be sure to contact the rescue operation, explain why you are handing over your snake and provide any necessary documentation concerning shots and medical care. You also may be required to provide any housing units or enclo-sures so that the snake has a safe place to stay and the rescue opera-tion doesn't have to buy supplies.

If you can't find a reptile rescue to give your snake to, consider giving it to a private owner. Place ads on Facebook advertising your inten-tion to give away your pet. Explain why you need to give it away and include a small rehoming fee if you think it's necessary. You may get a better response, though, if you can give the snake away along with everything the new pet owner needs to take care of it, such as the vivarium, heating mat, ointment and feeders.

Euthanasia

If your snake comes down with a disease and you cannot afford treat-ment or if the vet cannot treat your snake, it may be time to euthanize it. Take it to the vet for this process. The animal doctor has equip-ment that will allow this procedure to be performed safely and pain-lessly. Another reason you may look into euthanizing your pet is if you can no longer keep it and you have not successfully rehomed it. It seems cruel, but euthanasia is more humane than turning it out into the wild. If there's nothing physically wrong with your pet, though, you should only consider euthanizing it as a last resort.

CHAPTER SUMMARY

In this chapter, we have learned:

- When to rehome your pet snake

- When to euthanize your pet corn snake
- Why rehoming or euthanizing is better than turning out into the wild

IN THE NEXT CHAPTER, you will learn:

- Where to learn more about corn snakes

CHAPTER TWELVE: RECAP

Preparing to have a new pet corn snake takes some research and preparation. You can't just buy them, put them into an aquarium, walk away and expect them to become happy healthy well-adjusted pets. Like with most pets, you have to make the proper preparations in order to successfully keep them as pets.

LET'S review what we've learned:

OBTAINING YOUR CORN SNAKE:

- Obtain your snake from a reputable breeder, pet shop, or rehoming organization
- Do not buy a wild-caught snake
- Handle the snake before you buy it - if they don't allow you, don't buy the snake

- Have a general knowledge of venomous and non-venomous species - it's not likely one will be sold for the other, but it's still good to know the difference so that you aren't afraid of the snakes you encounter

PROPER ENCLOSURE:

- Keep the snake in a glass or plastic enclosure, unless you are an experienced reptile owner and know how to make another container or setup work
- Make sure the pet cannot escape
- Make sure the area is properly warmed and cooled
- A heating mat with a thermostat is probably the easiest to install and regulate
- Make sure the pet has plenty of water to soak in, absorbent substrate, a humid hide, a dry hide, as well as something rough to help them scrape off dead skin during shedding
- Make sure the enclosure is big enough to allow the pet to stretch out completely in the tank
- Try to make the conditions within the enclosure closely mimic the conditions in their natural habitat
- If you are using other live organisms, like springtails for a bioactive environment, make sure you get the conditions right

FEEDING:

- Do not feed live rodents to small or young snakes, as they may bite them and easily injure them
- Consider feeding your snake with feeding tongs so it doesn't associate your hand with food
- Get all of the information you can about your new snake's previous diet. Some snakes do not like change and may refuse to eat if it's a lot different from what they are used to eating
- If your snake refuses to eat for more than two weeks, take it to a vet - it may be sick
- Corn snakes eat rodents in the wild - do not feed them anything else

CARE:

- Handle your new snake often so that it gets used to being held - if you refuse to hold it because it may bite you, that may just encourage it to continue to act aggressively toward you
- Make sure you clean the enclosure regularly
- Watch out for signs of health problems, like scale rot, problems shedding, neurological issues, ticks, mites and loss of appetite

MEDICAL CARE:

- Shop around for a vet that specializes in reptiles

- Make sure your pet gets all the necessary checkups
- If something doesn't look right, take your pet in to get care

BECOMING AN ENTHUSIAST:

- Reptile expos are great places to learn more about your pet, as well as meet people who are more experienced snake owners, buy a snake and learn about advanced handling and care
- You can also find quality information about your animals on the internet, provided you know how to look for it

BREEDING AND SELLING:

- Never catch wild specimens to breed or sell
- Make sure you have the right equipment needed for breeding
- Make sure you have the right permits or licenses to sell reptiles if required

REHOMING:

- To prevent wild breeding and the introduction of invasive species, rehome your pet if you are not able to take care of it - don't just turn it out into the wild

- If your circumstances change, don't be afraid to rehome your pet - here are organizations and people who would give your pet a decent home if you become unable to care for it
- If you can't find an option for rehoming it or giving it to someone who can care for it, consider getting it euthanized - don't let it enter the local wild population

WHERE TO LEARN MORE

YOUTUBE

THERE'S a lot of helpful information about corn snakes on YouTube. I recommend you check out the many informational videos as one of your first steps in learning more about corn snake care. There are videos covering many different topics. For instance, if you were having trouble figuring out how to set up a properly heated enclosure using an under-the-tank heating pad, there are videos that will walk you through the process step by step, from where and how to stick the heating pad so that it doesn't create an inconvenience later to how to plug it in to a thermostat to monitor heat changes.

THERE ARE ALSO videos on how to treat your snake for mites, burns and bacterial infection, as well as videos on sexing snakes and breeding. The video libraries created by dedicated reptile enthusiasts may prove to be an invaluable resource as you continue your corn snake care journey. When searching for YouTube videos on how to properly care for corn snakes, look for videos that are of good quality and produced by a specialist with a lot of in-depth knowledge about reptiles. These videos will be less frustrating to new reptile owners looking for information because they will be of professional quality and are likely to not have a non-professional snake owner rambling about his or her experiences caring for a pet snake.

WHILE IT IS true that amateur blogs can be helpful when learning about snake care, you might want to avoid them unless you aren't looking for information and are just more interested in hearing about another's experience caring for snakes. Amateur blogs can get off-topic and waste time with irrelevant information. For example, you may click on a blog about a vet trip, but you may end up having to listen to the person blogging ramble about a pet dog or tell stories about a pet cat or turtle before you hear anything about the snake or learn any relevant information. Listening to a blog like this is fine if you've got some free time and just want to learn about another snake owner's experiences, but it may make you feel impatient if you clicked on the blog expecting to receive relevant information about an illness your snake may be experiencing.

HOW TO FIND **Good Quality Videos**

GOOD QUALITY informational videos about snake care are fairly easy to come by thanks to good search algorithms. To further avoid amateur blogs, though, search for specific rather than general topics. For example, instead of searching for the words "vet trip with pet corn snakes", consider searching "corn snakes vet care 101". It's even better if you can describe what you are searching for in more precise terms, such as "scale rot in corn snakes". Typing in more precise search terms is likely to bring you to the information you want instead of wasting your time with irrelevant information and potentially increasing your frustration by making an already tense situation a little worse.

YOU MAY ALSO WANT to subscribe to videos by reptile and snake rescue organizations. Rescue organizations tend to put out engaging accurate factual reptile care content. The videos also tend to be professional and don't waste time getting to the point. That's the difference between watching a video by a seasoned professional, like a reptile educator, and an amateur, like some young teenager who is trying to walk us through the experience of owning a pet corn snake but may not yet possess the experience or video editing skills necessary to give us a worthwhile experience.

ANY BASIC PIECE of information you want to know about snake care may also be available from pet shop blogs. Pet shops, like professional rescue organizations, are staffed by experts who can answer most questions about basic pet snake care. The internet, fortunately, has videos made by reputable pet shop keepers regarding questions you may have about your animal. Be sure, however, to view multiple videos from multiple reputable sources, especially if the information presented is not clear the first time you hear it or if you feel like you've heard contradictory information. The presenter may have been describing different products than what you thought the presenter was describing.

LEARNING **How To Use New Equipment**

SEARCH FOR "CORN snake tank set up" or, if you know what you want to search for specifically, search for those terms. Let's say you want to search for "heating mat" or "heating pad" for corn snakes. If you don't already know what kind of heating pad you want to use, begin by typing in something like "heating pad for corn snakes". This should bring up various heating pad options. Then, type something like "how to use the Reptitherm heating pad." Among your first few choices should be a list of popular videos. Click on one video and begin watching. Watch two or three videos to get a clear picture of how to use the equipment. Watching two or three different videos by different presenters can help you get an idea of the best way to use the equipment. For example, the heating mat comes with an adhesive on it to allow you to easily stick it to the tank, but you may not want to do this for a number of reasons.

- If your snake is going to grow, you may want to move the heat source when you transfer your snake to its new home
- The heat mat may get too hot and damage the glass or plastic
- The heat mat may get damaged due to getting too hot

MAKING **Your Own Videos**

TO SUCCESSFULLY MAKE reptile videos that people want to watch, first decide what you are going to talk about. Is it going to be an informational blog that kind of meanders around and covers various topics? Is it going to be a focused how-to video? Is it going to be a "shared experience" video? Next, decide on your topic. Deciding on your topic will better help you focus on what you want to talk about. People don't like watching videos where the presenter can't seem to make up his or her mind. Then, take a step back and watch several well-made videos on the topic. Watch with a pencil and a piece of paper in hand. Try to figure out why the videos you are watching work for their intended purpose. How's the pacing? The camera angles? How much are they talking? Is the presenter's message clear?

ONCE YOU'VE FOUND some videos that had interesting content and you've taken notes on them, create an outline for yourself and plan your video according to it. Write a practice script for your chosen topic and practice talking to an imaginary audience before you start recording. Make sure you have a good camera that will create a crisp picture. Some viewers do not like a shaky picture or unclear focus, so make sure you don't have that problem before you make your video. Practice taking short videos before filming. If you want to, you can also just make the video and then voice over your own actions.

YOUTUBE CHANNEL SUGGESTIONS

- Snake Discovery
- Clint's Reptiles
- Go Herping

SCIENTIFIC ARTICLES **And Blogs**

ANOTHER FAIRLY GOOD source of online information on corn snakes are scientific articles and blogs published by reputable sources like vets, colleges, and government websites.

SCIENTIFIC BLOGS

THESE CAN BE A FAIRLY good source of information if you know what topic you are looking for. If, for example, you want to re-read how to sex a snake or check for scale rot, you can type those phrases in as search terms and look up the information and read up on it to refresh your memory. Looking up information on blogs is sometimes faster than watching an informational video. You can also find more in-depth specific information as long as you know what you are looking for, to begin with.

REMEMBER, though, only trust reputable sources. Personal blogs and even blogs from supposedly well-meaning organizations, like the humane society, may have misleading information, politically charged articles and propaganda. It's good to know about the issues affecting animals, but it's also good to keep in mind that personal blogs and blogs from certain animal care non-profits may not be the most objective source of animal care information.

READING PERSONAL BLOGS, especially those with a political slant, may only serve to disappoint or anger you and that's not what you're trying to accomplish. For example, reading a politically slanted article with misinformation about snake owners might make you upset with either the article or your fellow snake owners who are not as conscientious. Don't get mad - just make sure you aren't like the people the articles decry.

Your animal may have less of a chance of becoming an invasive species where you live if you never release it. Mistakes happen, but do everything you can to mitigate risks and care for your animals and the environment by ensuring that your snake stays in captivity and does not breed in the wild. Don't listen to the ignorance that decries snake ownership as something "evil" because there's a potential risk to the environment if your snake gets loose. These are scare tactics. Know the real risks, keep abreast of the real issues, but don't give in to the mudslinging or pet shaming. As long as you are a responsible owner, you have little to worry about.

THIS IS one reason why reptile hobbyist advocacy groups exist - to educate the public and cut through the rhetoric and lies some organizations, well-meaning or not, spread about snakes and their owners. That's why it's important to attend reptile expos and join other reptile enthusiasts who can help you inform the general public of the real issues.

SCIENTIFIC ARTICLES

ANOTHER SOURCE of information is scientific articles published by vets and colleges. These have information and case studies on animals and can provide a wealth of information if you have time to read them and know what you're looking for. They sometimes contain a bit of jargon or industry-specific terminology, but if you can get past that, they are a way to learn much more about your pet and may also be a way for you to start educating yourself beyond the basics. You can read studies about many potential topics pertaining to your snake, such as "reptiles and Ph and why you should never use distilled water in an enclosure".

THIS, along with regularly caring for your animal, will help you appear to be the expert. You'll start being able to answer questions and understand your veterinarian when he uses specific terms and you'll have a better lexicon to communicate with your fellow reptile enthusiasts. Eventually, if you ever decide to educate people on corn snake ownership, reading articles and blogs will potentially make you more knowledgeable than the average hobbyist owner and make you appear to be an authority on the subject.

SCIENTIFIC ARTICLES **And Blogs Suggestions**

- Vetstreet
- Prescott Animal Hospital
- National Institute of Health
- Oxford University Press
- Science Direct
- Reptile Magazine

REPTILE OWNERSHIP **And Care Forums**

JOINING online forums is a great place to connect with fellow reptile owners and learn about corn snakes from experienced handlers. They can also be a great resource of information for specific problems that may be afflicting your snake. You can get tips for what to do if your snake won't eat, how to use a heating mat or a basking lamp, and generally how to give your corn snake the best possible care. You can also post links to pictures, blogs, and videos, and just talk about how much you love the animal.

FORUM SUGGESTIONS

- Fellow Herper
- Reptile Magazine

CHAPTER SUMMARY

In this chapter, we learned:

- Options for learning more about corn snakes online
- How to make good online videos about corn snakes

FINAL WORDS

That's almost everything you need to know to select and raise a pet corn snake. If you've found this book helpful, consider leaving a five-star rating on Amazon to let everyone else know how you enjoyed it and how helpful it was. As a closing exercise, please take out a piece of paper and write down the five most helpful things you've learned from reading this book. When you are finished, come back and continue reading.

Example -

What I learned from reading this book:

- Corn snakes are easy snakes to keep
- They eat mainly mice
- Veterinarians recommend frozen-thawed to live mice
- To keep from burning your snake, you should get a thermostat
- It is important to keep the conditions inside of the enclosure hospitable for your snake, with proper humidity, correct temperature, etc.

Now, post the five things you learned from reading this book in the comments on Amazon. If you have children who are going to own corn snakes, allow them to read this book, or read it with them and allow them to complete the "what I learned" exercise, as well.

Enjoy your new pet!

ACKNOWLEDGMENTS

Image Credits: Shutterstock.com

Lightning Source UK Ltd.
Milton Keynes UK
UKHW020348030222
398101UK00006B/141